· TROPHIES ·

Intervention Practice Book

Kindergarten

Teacher's Edition

Harcourt

Orlando   Boston   Dallas   Chicago   San Diego

Visit *The Learning Site!*
www.harcourtschool.com

ISBN 0-15-329345-4

3 4 5 6 7 8 9 10   054   10 09 08 07 06 05 04 03

CONTENTS

Name_____

Directions: Have children trace each letter. Then have them look at each picture and circle the letter that stands for the beginning sound of the picture name.

Name_____

_____

a

_____

a

Responses will vary.

_____

a

Directions: Read each phrase and have children trace the words. Then have them trace the word *a* again and draw a picture in the box to make a new phrase.

© Harcourt

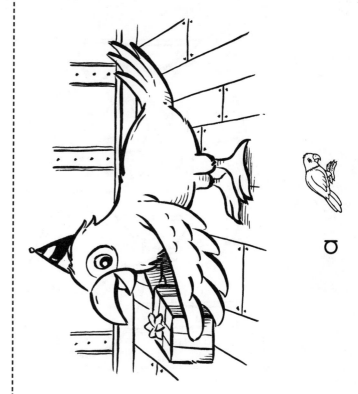

A

a

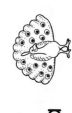

a

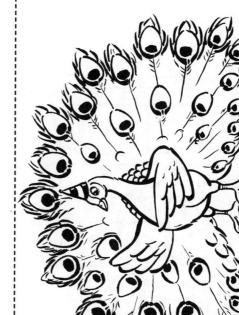

Fold

Fold

Harcourt

Dear Family Members,

This Take-Home Book contains words your child is learning. After reading the story with your child, encourage him or her to read it to you. Then help your child make an invitation to an imaginary party he or she would like to have.

3

8

6

a

a

a

— Fold —

✄

— Fold —

a

a

Harcourt

✄ ✄

4 **Practice Readers**

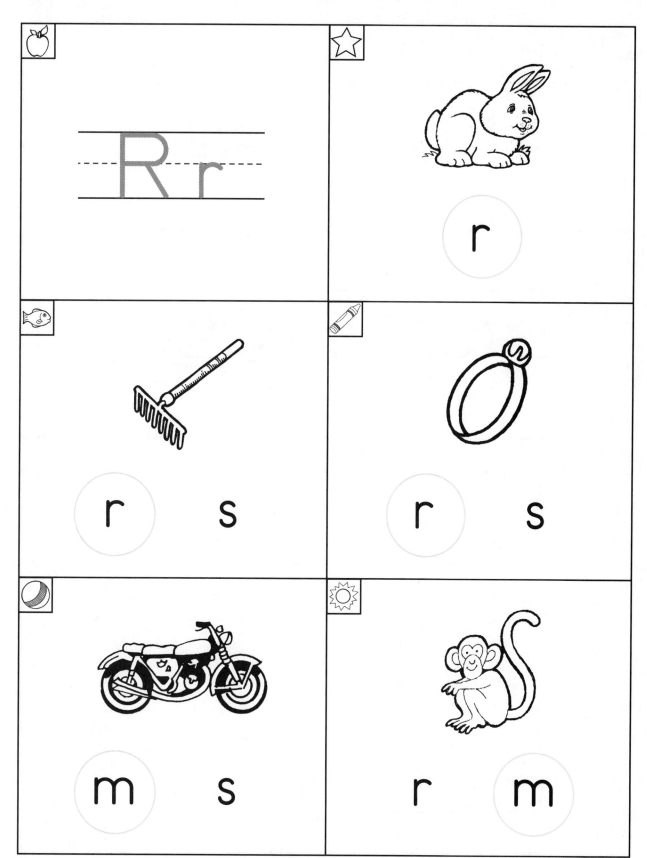

Directions: Have children trace each letter. Then have them look at each picture and circle the letter that stands for the beginning sound of each picture name.

🍎

_____

- - - - - - my - - - - -

⭐

_____

- - - - - - my - - - - -

🐟

Responses will vary.

_____

- - - - - - my - - - - -

Directions: Read each phrase and have children trace *my*. Then have them trace the word again and draw a picture in the box to make a new phrase.

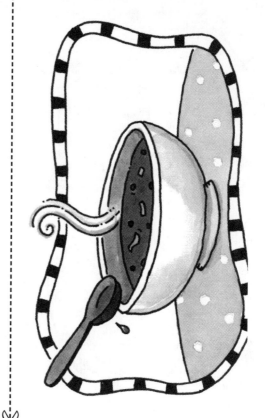

My

my

Fold

Fold

Dear Family Members,

This Take-Home Book contains words that your child is learning. After reading the story with your child, encourage him or her to read it to you. Then have your child name some of his or her favorite lunch foods. Invite him or her to draw pictures of the foods.

my

Harcourt

8

3

9

Directions: Help children cut and fold the book.

my

my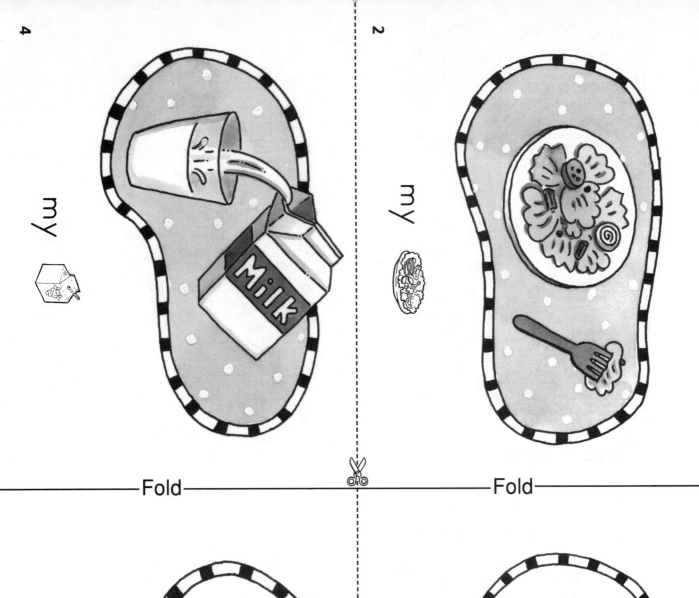

—Fold—

✂

—Fold—

my

Mmm!

Harcourt

✂

✂

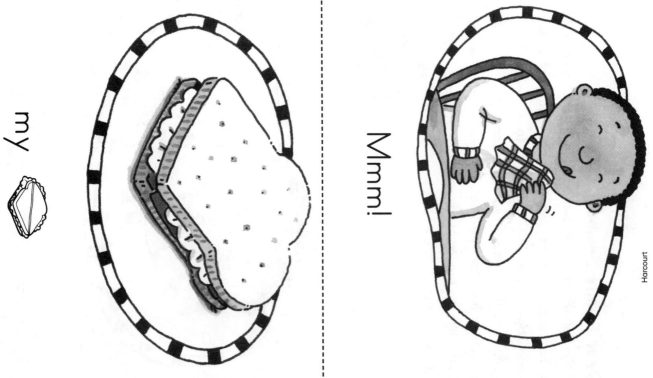

Name_____

t (m)	t m
t s	t (m)
t (s)	(t) m

Directions: Have children trace each letter. Then have them look at each picture and circle the letter that stands for the beginning sound of each picture name.

Name_____

the

the

Responses will vary.

the

© Harcourt

Directions: Read each phrase and have children trace *the.* Then have them
trace the word *the* again and draw a picture in the box to make a new phrase.

The Zoo

the

Fold

Dear Family Members,

This Take-Home Book contains words that your child is learning. After reading the story with your child, encourage him or her to read it to you. Then have your child name some of his or her favorite zoo animals. Take turns telling facts you both know about any of the animals.

Harcourt

the

Directions: Help children cut and fold the book.

Practice Readers 11

4

the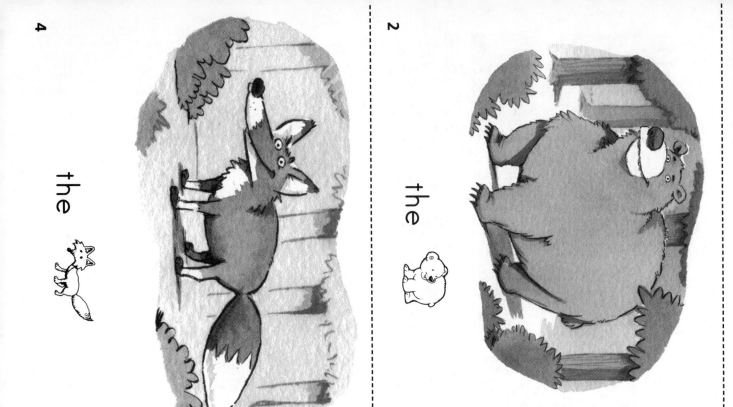

2

the

Fold

Fold ✄

the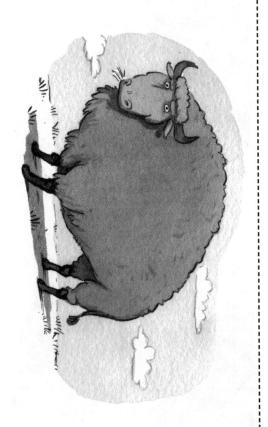

the

5

7

Name_____

I like  .

Responses will vary.

I like .

Directions: Read each sentence and have children trace the words *I* and *like*. Then have them trace the words *I like* again and draw a picture in the box to make a new sentence.

Directions: Have children trace each letter. Then have them circle the letter
that stands for the beginning sound of each picture name.

© Harcourt

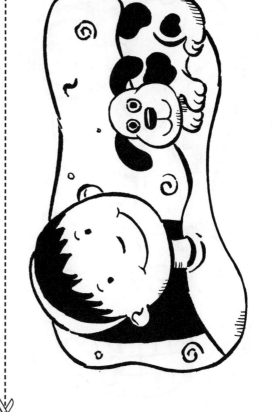

I
Like

Fold

I like my .

Fold

Dear Family Members,

This Take-Home Book contains words that your child is learning. After reading the story with your child, encourage him or her to read it to you. Then play a birthday-party game. In a gift box, hide a familiar object. Give your child hints to help him or her find the object.

8

I like my .

6

Directions: Help children cut and fold the book.

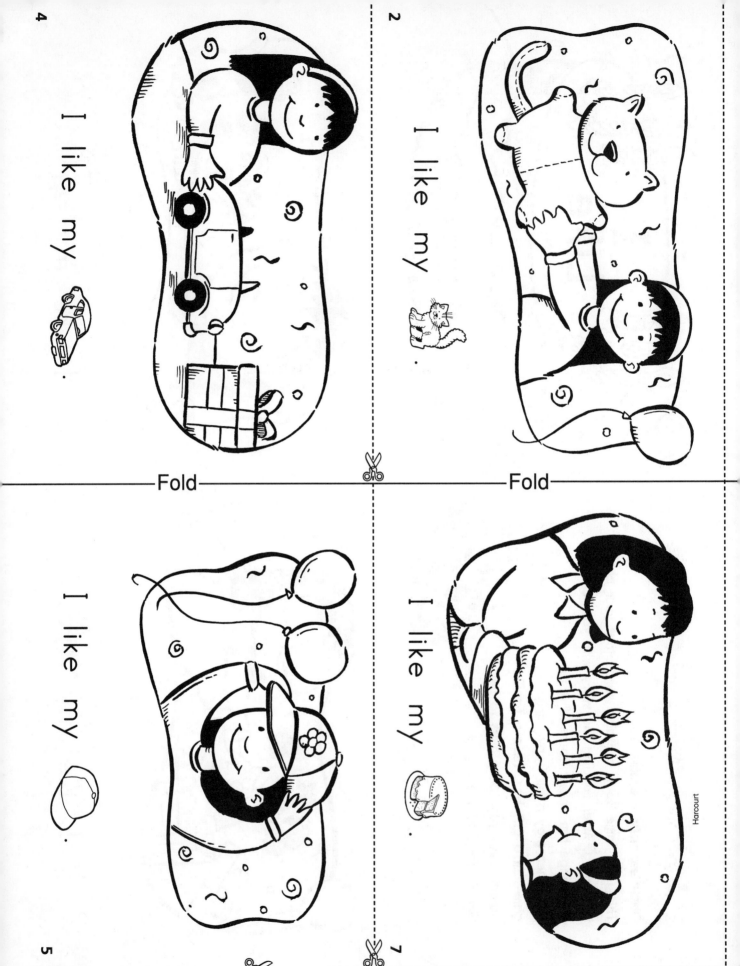

4

I like my _____ .

2

I like my _____ .

Fold

Fold

I like my _____ .

I like my _____ .

5

7

16 Practice Readers

Aa

a

a   m

a   m

a   m

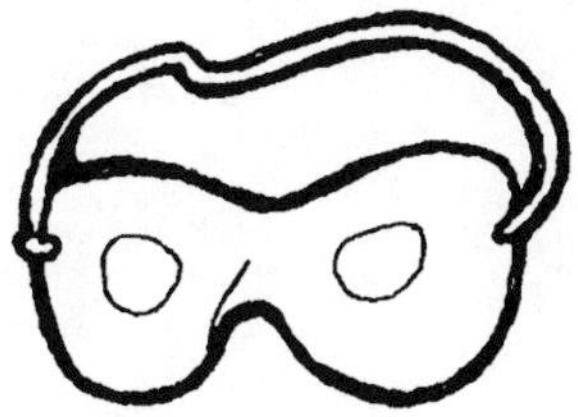

a   m

Directions: Have children trace each letter. Then have them circle the letter
that stands for the beginning sound of each picture name.

© Harcourt

I like  .

Responses will vary.

I like .

Directions: Read the sentence and have children trace the words. Then have them trace the words
I like again and draw a picture in the box to complete the sentence.

Name_____

map

cap

Pam

cat

✂

map | cat | cap | Pam

Directions: Have children trace the words at the bottom of the page and cut them out. Tell them to paste the word that names each picture.

• cat

• cap

• mat

• map

Directions: Have children trace each letter. Then have them name the picture and draw a line from the picture to the picture name.

Name_____

I like my  .

☆

Responses will vary.

I like my _____ .

I like my _____ .

Directions: Read the sentence and have children trace the words. Then have them trace the words *I like my* again and draw a picture in the box to complete the sentence.

© Harcourt

Name_____

Directions: Have children trace the letters at the bottom of the page and cut them out. Tell them to paste the letter in the first box if it stands for the beginning sound of each picture name or paste it in the second box if it stands for the ending sound of each picture name.

Responses will vary.

We go .

We go .

We go .

Directions: Read the sentence, "We go sailing," and have children trace the words *We go*. Then have them trace the sentence again and draw a picture to complete each sentence.

Directions: Have children trace each letter. Then have them circle the letter that stands for the beginning sound of each picture name.

We Can Go!

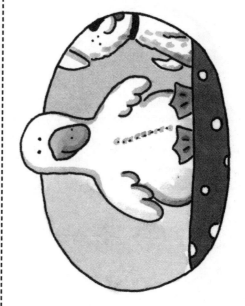

 can go.

Dear Family Members,

This Take-Home Book contains words your child is learning. After reading the story with your child, encourage him or her to read it to you. Talk about other toys the girl might put in her wagon.

Harcourt

8

 can go.

6

4

can go.

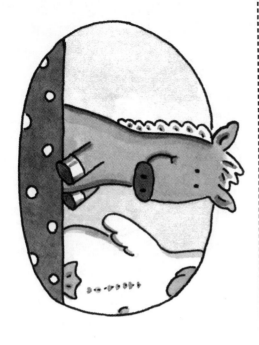

2

can go.

— Fold — ✂ — Fold —

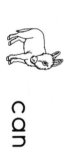

can go.

5

We can go!

Harcourt

7

Name_____

Directions: Have children trace each letter. Explain that the sounds /a/ and /p/ together are used to make lots of words. Then have them draw a line from the picture to the word that names the picture.

I like the  .

Responses will vary.

I like the .

I like the .

Directions: Read the sentence and have children trace the words. Then have children trace each sentence and draw a picture to complete it.

© Harcourt

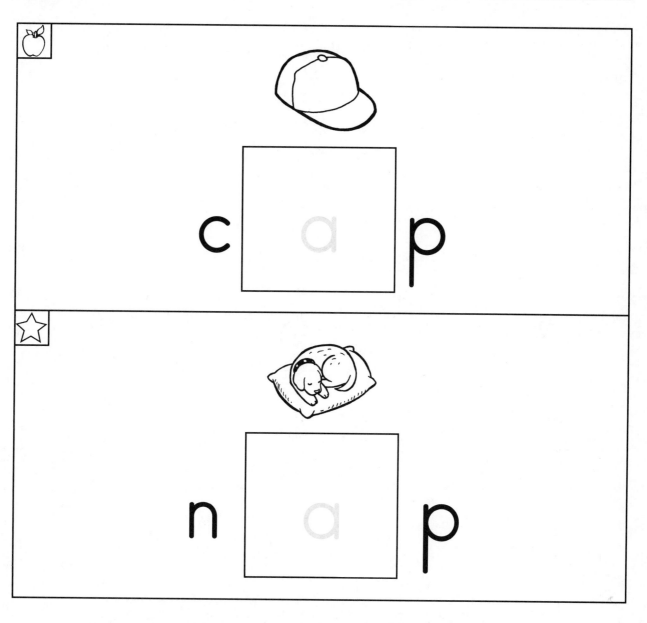

Directions: Have children trace the letters in the boxes at the bottom of the page and then cut them out. Tell them to paste the missing letter in each word and read the words together.

Name_____

nap

tap

cap

Directions: Have children name the pictures, trace the letters, and blend the sounds to read the words. Then have them follow the same steps and draw a picture of the word they read.

We like  .

Responses will vary.

I like •

I like •

Directions: Read the sentence at the top of the page. Have children trace the words. Then read the words at the bottom and have them draw a picture to complete each sentence.

At the Zoo

I like the .

Harcourt

Dear Family Members,

This Take-Home Book contains words that your child is learning. After reading the story with your child, encourage him or her to read it to you. Then ask your child to name his or her favorite animal at the zoo.

8

I like the  .

6

Directions: Help children cut and fold the book.

Practice Readers **35**

I like the .

I like the .

Fold

Fold

I like the .

We like the .

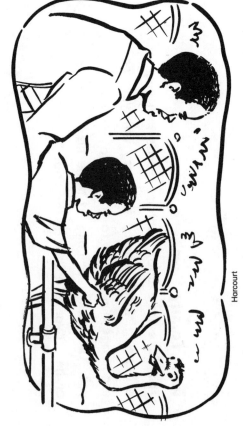

Harcourt

Name_____

c   s

d   g

n   m

s   p

g   t

r   n

Directions: Help children identify each picture. Have them trace the letter that stands for the beginning sound of the picture name.

We go on.

Responses will vary.

We like to go.

Directions: Read the sentences with children. Point out new words *on* and *to*. Then have them trace the words and draw a picture to go with the second sentence.

© Harcourt

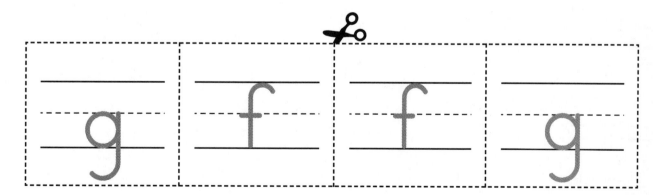

Directions: Have children trace the letters at the bottom of the page and cut them out. Help children identify the pictures. Then children match the letters with the beginning sound of each picture.

Name _____

I i

sit

i

i

mitt

sit

Directions: Have children trace the letters. Then help them identify each picture name and trace the beginning or medial letter.

Name_____

I sit on a 🪑 .

Responses will vary.

I sit on a .

Directions: Help children read the sentence before they trace the words. Then have children complete the sentence and draw a picture of their favorite place to sit.

p i [ ] g   h [ ] a t

t [ ] a g   s [ ] i t

✂

i   i   a   a

Directions: Have children trace the letters at the bottom of the page and cut them out. Help children identify the pictures. Then children paste *a* or *i* in the box to complete each picture name.

Name _____

pin   pan

_____

pat   pig

_____

tip   tag

_____

rag   rim

_____

Directions: Help children name each picture and read the word choices below each picture.
Then children circle the word that names the picture and write the word.

Name_____

I like to go  .

Responses will vary.

I like to go   .

Directions: Read the sentence with children and have them trace the words. Then have them trace the words *I like to go* and draw a picture in the box to complete the sentence.

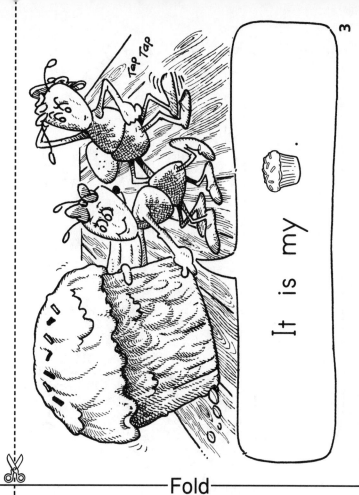

It is my 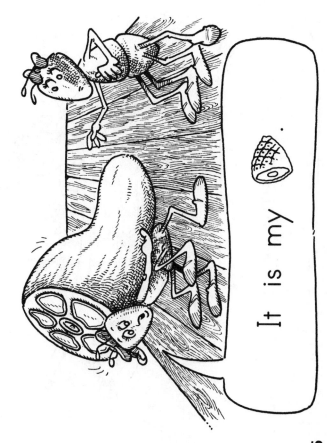 .

---Fold--- ✂ ---Fold---

Dear Family Members,
This Take-Home Book contains words that your child is learning. After reading the story with your child, encourage him or her to read it to you. Then make a list of the rhyming words in the story and have your child name some more rhyming words.

It is my 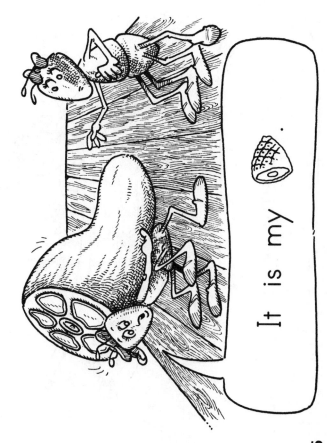 .

Directions: Help children cut and fold the book.

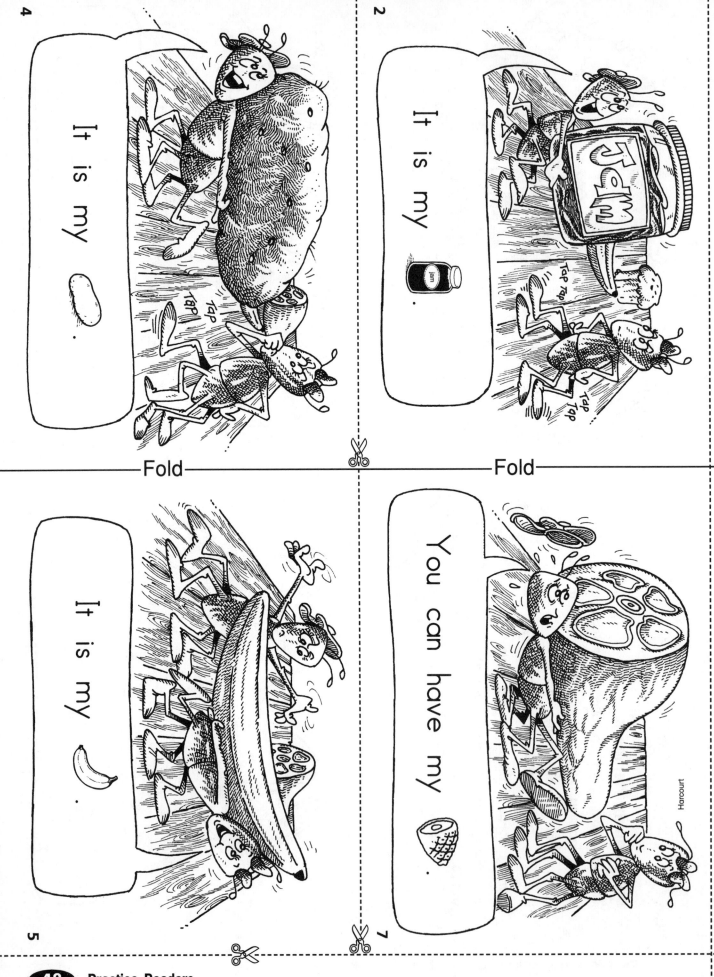

You have .

Responses will vary.

You have 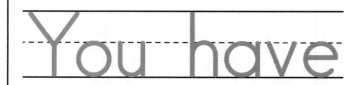 .

Directions: Read the sentence with children and have them trace the words. Then have children read the words *You have* again, trace them, and draw a picture in the box to complete the sentence.

Name_____

Directions: Have children trace each letter. Then have them circle the letter that stands for the beginning sound of each picture.

© Harcourt

The

You have a .

3

Harcourt

Dear Family Members,

This Take-Home Book contains words that your child is learning. After reading the story with your child, encourage him or her to read it to you. Talk about other things Hippo might add to his house.

8

"CREAK"

You have a .

6

Directions: Help children cut and fold the book.

Practice Readers 51

You have a .

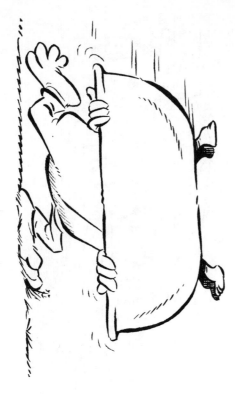

2

You have a 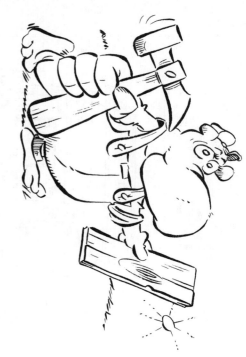.

—Fold—

✂

Fold—

You have a .

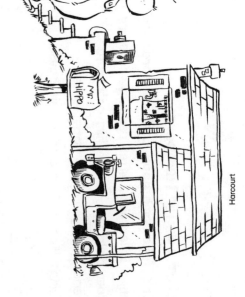

Harcourt

You have a .

7

lip   lap

_____

dig   pig

_____

tip   hip

_____

pin   pan

_____

Directions: Help children name each picture. Then have them read the words
and circle the word that names the picture. Finally children write the word.

Name_____

I have my  .

We like .

Directions: Read the sentence with children and have them trace the words. Then have them read and trace the words at the bottom and draw a picture to complete the sentence.

You Have It

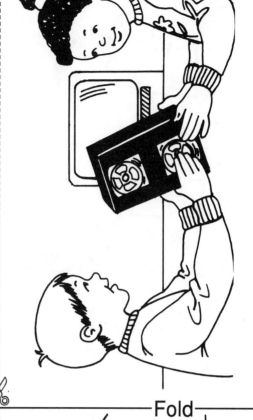

I like the 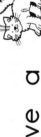.

Fold

Dear Family Members,

This Take-Home Book contains words your child is learning. After reading the story with your child, encourage him or her to read it to you. Then make a list of your child's favorite things.

Harcourt

You have a .

Directions: Help children cut and fold the book.

You have a .

You have a .

—Fold—

Fold

I like the .

I like the .

Harcourt

Name_____

rip (circled)   rig

_____

_____

sip   sit (circled)

_____

_____

hip   lip (circled)

_____

_____

pig (circled)   pit

_____

_____

Directions: Help children name the pictures and read the words. Then have children circle the word that names the picture and write the word.

Name_____

I like to go.

Responses will vary.

I like to go

•

Directions: Read the sentences with children and have them trace the words. Then have children draw a picture to show a place they like to go.

I Have

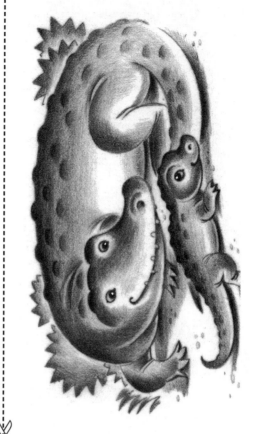

I have my ____ .

Fold

Dear Family Members,

This Take-Home Book contains words that your child is learning. After reading the story with your child, encourage him or her to read it to you. Then start an animal dictionary together. Help your child choose an animal. Have him or her draw the animal and label it.

Harcourt

Fold

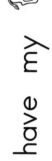

I have my ____ .

Directions: Help children cut and fold the book.

Practice Readers **59**

I have my  .

I have my  .

—Fold—

Fold—

I have my 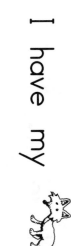 .

I have my .

I have my  .

Harcourt

What do you do?

Responses will vary.

What do you do?

Directions: Read the question with children and have them read and trace the words. Then have them read and trace the words at the bottom and draw a picture in the box to answer the question.

© Harcourt

Name_____

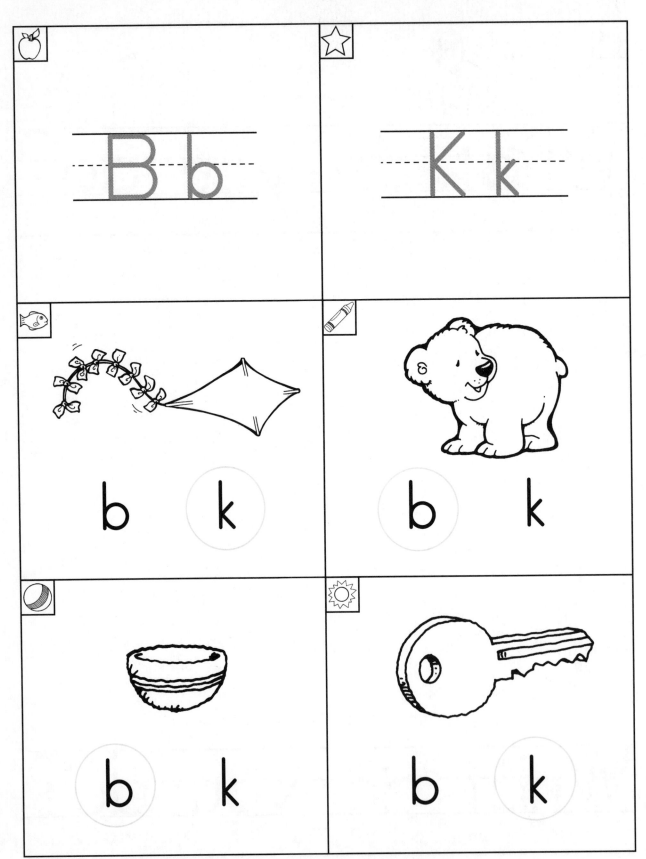

Directions: Have children trace each letter. Help them identify the picture names before they circle the letter that stands for the beginning sound of each picture name.

© Harcourt

Can I Do It?

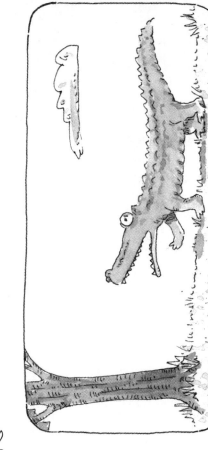

What can I do?

3

Harcourt

Dear Family Members,

This Take-Home Book contains words that your child is learning. After reading the story with your child, encourage him or her to read it to you. Then talk about other ways the animals may have gotten the kitten down from the tree.

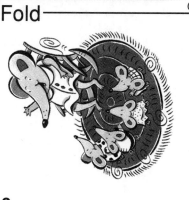

8

What can I do?

6

Directions: Help children cut and fold the book.

What can I do?

2

What can I do?

—Fold—

—Fold—

What can I do?

I can do it!

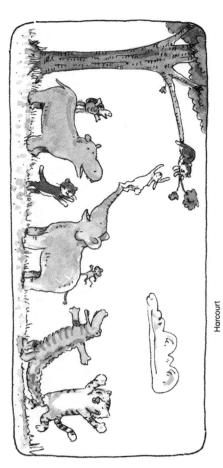

Harcourt

Name_____

🍎 Oo	⭐ Tt
🐟 ⓞ t	🖍 o ⓣ
⚪ pop ⓟⓞⓣ	☀️ ⓣⓞⓟ tot

Directions: Have children trace each letter. Next have them circle the letter that stands for the beginning sound of each picture name. Then have them circle the word that names the picture.

© Harcourt

Name _____

What is it?

It is a  .

Responses will vary.

What is it?

It is a .

Directions: Read the question and response with children and have them trace the words. Then have them read and trace the words again and write and draw the answer to the question.

Name _____

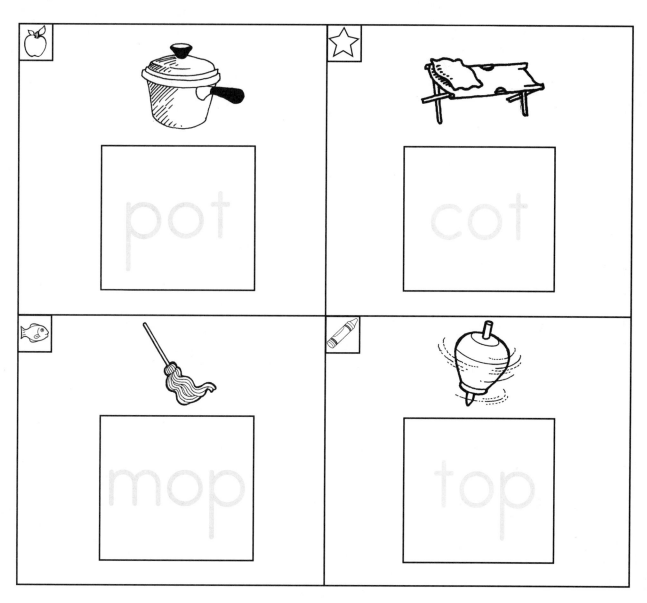

Directions: Have children trace and read the words at the bottom of the page and then cut them out. Tell them to paste the word that names each picture.

pit   pot

hot   hat

_____
- - - - - - - - - - - - - - - -
pot
_____

_____
- - - - - - - - - - - - - - - -
hat
_____

map   mop

top   tap

_____
- - - - - - - - - - - - - - - -
mop
_____

_____
- - - - - - - - - - - - - - - -
top
_____

Directions: Help children name the pictures and read the words. Then have them circle the word that names the picture and then write the word.

Name_____

What can hop?

Responses will vary.

It can hop.

Directions: Read the question with children and have them trace the words. Then have them trace the words for the response and draw a picture to go with the sentence.

Directions: Have children trace and read the words at the bottom of the page and then cut them out. Tell them to paste the word that names each picture.

© Harcourt

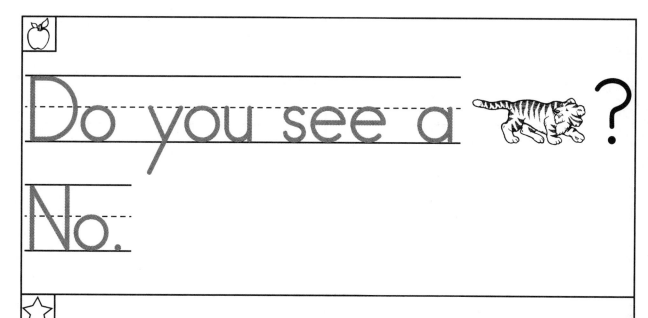

Do you see a ?

No.

Responses will vary.

What do you see?

Directions: Read the question and response with children and have them trace the words. Tell them to trace *no* if the answer to the question is no. Then have them read and trace the question and draw a picture showing what they see.

Ww

Xx

Directions: Have children trace the letters. Then identify the pictures with children. Have them write the beginning letter of the picture name.

© Harcourt

The

I see it on the ___.

Can you see a ___?

Harcourt

Dear Family Members,

This Take-Home Book contains words that your child is learning. After reading the story with your child, encourage him or her to read it to you. Then talk about animals that lay eggs.

Fold

Fold

3

6

8

Directions: Help children cut and fold the book.

Can you see a ?

Can you see a ?

I see it on the .

I see it on the .

Fold

Fold

Harcourt

f o x

b o x

m o p

p o t

d o g

s i x

Directions: Help children identify the pictures and say each picture name. Tell children to listen to the middle sound in the word and then write *i* or *o* to complete the word.

© Harcourt

It is a big box.

What do you see?

Responses will vary.

Directions: Help children read the sentences. Have them trace the words in the sentence. Tell them to draw a picture of something that could be in the box.

Name_____

Directions: Have children trace the words at the bottom of the page and cut them out. Have children paste the word in the boxes to name each picture.

The fox ran.

Responses will vary.

I see a big box.

Directions: Help children read the sentences. Then have children trace the words and draw a picture for each sentence.

Name _____

Do you see my ?

I see it.

Responses will vary.

Do you see one ?

I see it.

Directions: Help children read and trace the questions and responses. Tell them
to draw a picture showing where the bird is and where the flower is.

Directions: Have children trace the phonograms and cut them out. Help them identify the pictures. Have children paste the correct phonogram in each box to complete each picture name.

Come and look.

Look at the  .

We can go in it.

Responses will vary.

Directions: Help children trace and read the sentences. Then have them draw a picture to show who is in the boat.

Name_____

Directions: Have children trace each letter. Help them identify the pictures. Then have them circle the letter that stands for the beginning sound of each picture name.

© Harcourt

The Cap

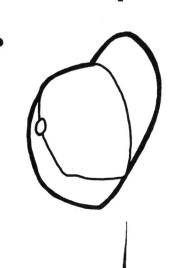

Look on the

Fold

Harcourt

Dear Family Members,

This Take-Home Book contains words that your child is learning. After reading the story with your child, encourage him or her to read it to you. Then talk about what to do if you lose something.

8

Fold

Can you see my 🧢 ?

6

Directions: Help children cut and fold the book.

4

Can you see my  ?

Can you see my  ?

Come look!

Harcourt

—Fold—

—Fold—

Look on the 🪑 .

hen

web

bed

jet

Directions: Help children blend and read the words. After they trace each phonogram, have them draw a line from each word to the picture it names.

to

to   top

have

have   hat

you

you   jet

come

cot   come

the

the   hen

do

do   to

Directions: Have children read and trace the words. Then have them circle the word that is the same as the word they traced.

© Harcourt

Name

jet

wet

net

pet

✂

wet | net | jet | pet

Directions: Have children trace the words at the bottom of the page and cut them out. Help children identify the pictures. Have children paste the correct word in the box to name each picture.

men   man

_____

- - - - - - - - - - - - - -

_____

pin   pen

_____

- - - - - - - - - - - - - -

_____

hen   ham

_____

- - - - - - - - - - - - - -

_____

tan   ten

_____

- - - - - - - - - - - - - -

_____

Directions: Help children identify the pictures and read the words. Then have children circle the word that names the picture and then write the word.

Come and look!

Look in the .

What do you see?

Responses will vary.

Directions: Read the sentences and question with children and have them trace them.
Then have them draw a picture to answer the question.

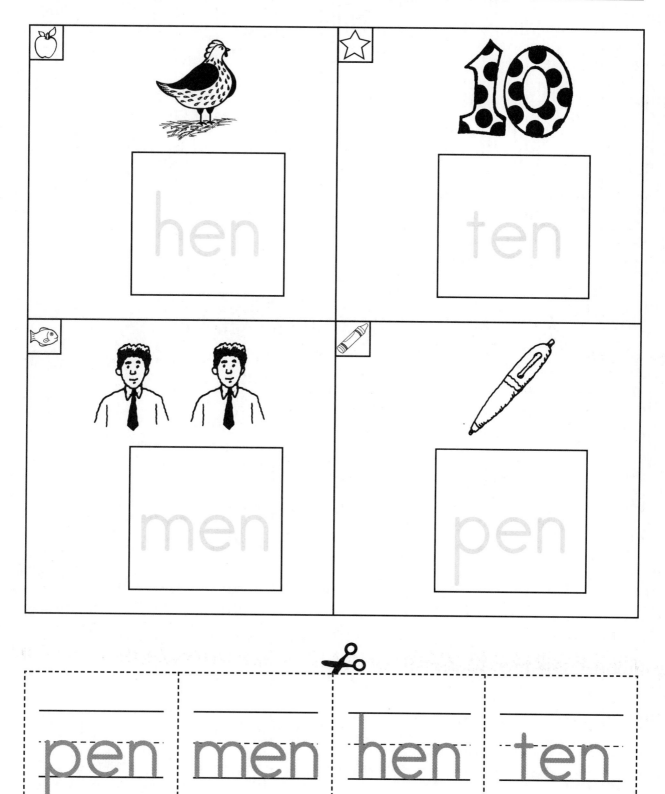

Directions: Have children trace the words and cut them out. Help children identify the pictures. Then have children paste the words to name each picture.

The is for the dog.

It is for me.

Directions: Read the sentence with children. Have them choose a picture to complete the sentence. Then have them read the sentence at the bottom and draw a picture to go with it.

Name

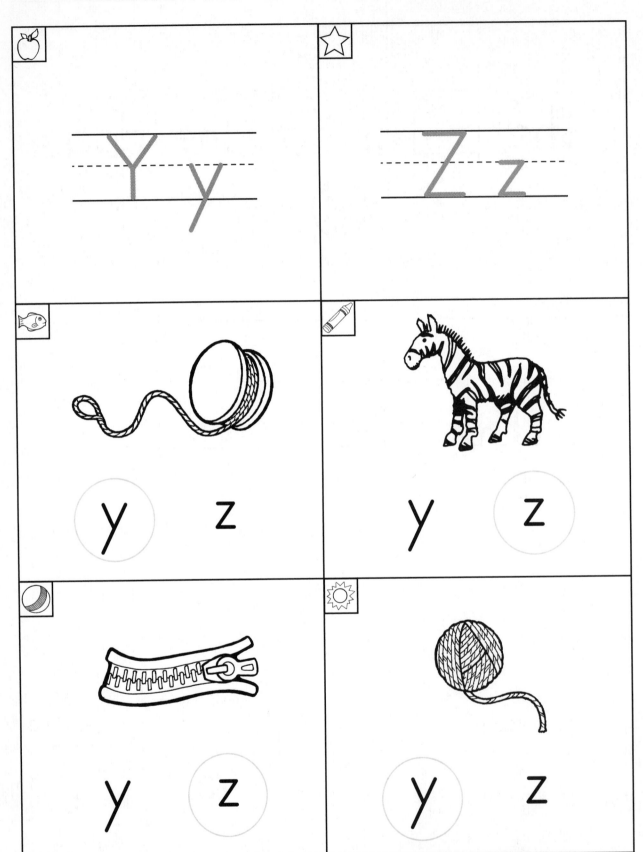

Directions: Have children trace the letters. Help them identify the pictures before they circle the letter that stands for the beginning sound of each picture name.

© Harcourt

What Do You Have for Me?

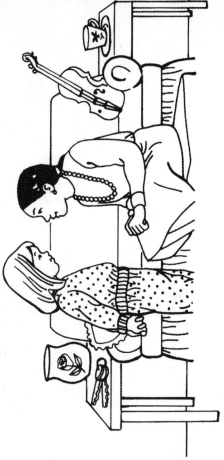

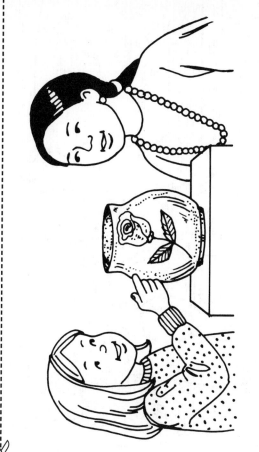

Is it for me?

Fold ✂ Fold

Dear Family Members,

This Take-Home Book contains words that your child is learning. After reading the story with your child, encourage him or her to read it to you. Then make a list of objects in your living room.

Is it for me?

8

6

Directions: Help children cut and fold the book.

4

Is it for me?

2

Is it for me?

Fold

Fold

What do you have?

5

I have a  for you.

7

Harcourt

bed

red

Ned

Directions: Have children trace the word bed and identify the picture. Then have them trace the next two words and draw a picture for each word.

Name

What can you get?

Responses will vary.

I can get a   .

Directions: Help children read the words before they trace them. Then have them draw a picture to complete the second sentence.

Come See

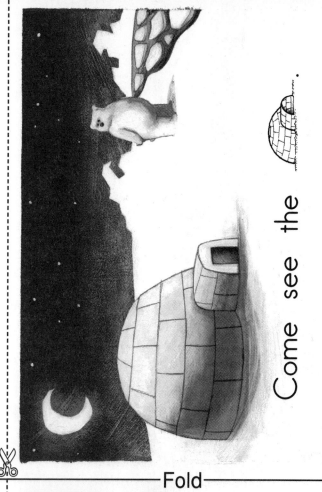

Come see the

Come see the ____ .

— Fold —

— Fold —

Dear Family Members,

This Take-Home Book contains words that your child is learning. After reading the story with your child, encourage him or her to read it to you. Then talk about what happens in winter in your neighborhood.

8

Come see the ____ .

6

Directions: Help children cut and fold the book.

Come see the).

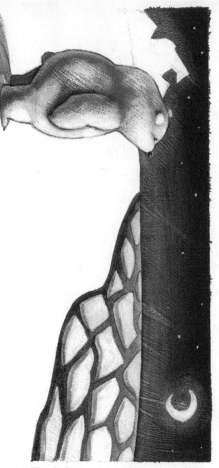

Come see the .

Fold

Fold

Come see the 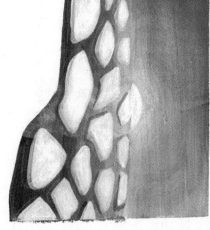 .

Come see the .

Harcourt

Name_____

bed

fed

Ted

Directions: Have children trace the word bed and identify the picture. Then have them trace and read the next two words and draw a picture for each word.

Is it for me?

Responses will vary.

Yes. It is for me.

Directions: Help children read the sentences before they trace them. Then have children draw a picture to go with the sentences.

Name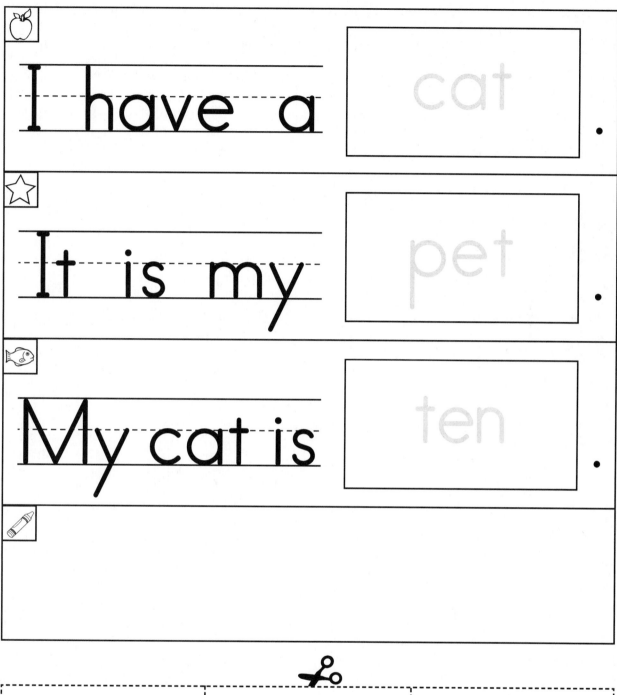

I have a | cat .

It is my | pet .

My cat is | ten .

✂

pet | ten | cat

Directions: Help children read the sentences and the words below. Have them trace the missing words and paste them in the appropriate sentences. Then have them draw a picture to go with the sentences.

Q q

Y y

q y

q y

q y

q y

Directions: Have children trace each letter. Then have them circle the letter that stands for the beginning sound in each picture name.

It is a little 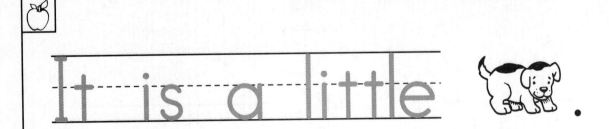 .

Responses will vary.

It is a little _____ .

Directions: Help children read each sentence before they trace the words.
Then have them draw a picture to complete the last sentence.

© Harcourt

We Like What We See

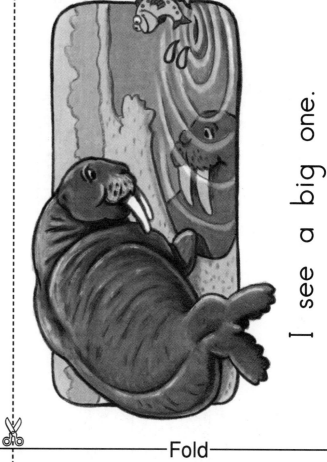

I see a big one.

Fold

Fold

Dear Family Members,

This Take-Home Book contains words that your child is learning. After reading the story with your child, encourage him or her to read it to you. Then make a list of all the places your child can see his or her reflection.

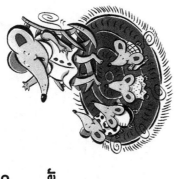

8

I see a little one.

Directions: Help children cut and fold the book.

I see a big one.

I see a little one.

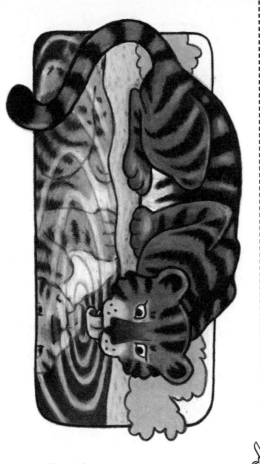

Fold

Fold

I see a big one.

We like what we see.

Harcourt

cut

nut

hut

Directions: Have children trace and read each word. Help them identify each picture and then draw a line from the word to the picture it names.

Name _____

I have a little  .

I have a little .

Responses will vary.

We can have a  .

Directions: Read each sentence with children before they trace the words. Then have them draw a picture in the box to describe the sentence.

cup

hut

cut

nut

hut nut cut cup

Directions: Have children trace and read the words at the bottom of the page and then cut them out. Tell them to paste the word that names each picture.

sun   sat

not   nut

bin   bun

run   rub

Directions: Help children identify the pictures and read the words before they circle the word that names the picture. Then have children write the word they circled.

One little bug.

 One big bug.

 One little or big hug!

Responses will vary.

Directions: Help children read the sentences and complete them. Then have children draw a picture of the two bugs hugging.

Directions: Have children trace and read the words at the bottom of the page and then cut them out. Tell them to paste the word that names each picture.

Name_____

(bug) but	jig (jug)
_____	_____
----bug----	----jug----
_____	_____
not (nut)	(mug) mud
_____	_____
----nut----	----mug----
_____	_____

Directions: Have children name the pictures, circle the words that name the pictures and then write the words.

Name_____

Here are my 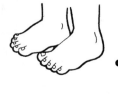.

Responses will vary, but be sure
children begin their sentences
with *Here are my*.

_____

- -

_____

Directions: Help children read the sentence before they trace the words. Then have them draw a picture of two or more things they have and write a sentence to go with it.

We Are Here

3

The 🐱 is here.

Fold — ✂ — Fold

Dear Family Members,

This Take-Home Book contains words that your child is learning. After reading the story with your child, encourage him or her to read it to you. Then talk about different kinds of boats you might see on the ocean.

Harcourt

8

The 🐰 is here.

6

Directions: Help children cut and fold the book.

4

The is here.

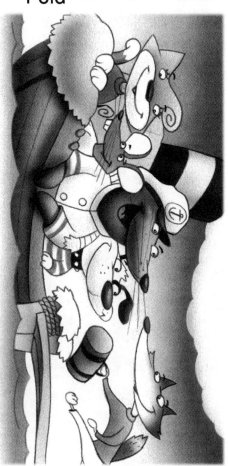

2

The is here.

Fold

The  is here.

5

We are here!

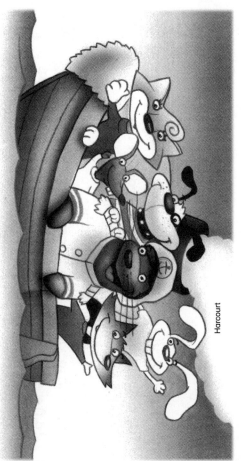

Harcourt

7

Fold

124 Practice Readers

Name_____

(rug)   rag

sub   (sun)

net   (nut)

(bug)   beg

Directions: Have children identify the pictures, read the words, and circle the words that name the pictures. Then have children write the words.

© Harcourt

Name _____

Are you here?

Responses will vary.

Here I am!

Directions: Read each sentence and have children trace the words. Then have them draw a picture of themselves.

© Harcourt

Name _____

Directions: Have children trace and read the words at the bottom of the page and then cut them out. Tell them to paste the word that names each picture.

i   **a**

i   o

o   e

u   e

o   **a**

u   i

Directions: Have children identify each picture name and circle the letter that
stands for the middle sound of each picture name.

Name_____

We go to the .

We see the .

Responses will vary.

We see the .

Directions: Help children read each sentence before they trace the words. Then have them draw a picture to complete the last sentence.

jug

dog

hat

six

hat   six   dog   jug

Directions: Have children trace and read the words at the bottom of the page and then cut them out. Tell them to paste the word that names each picture.

© Harcourt

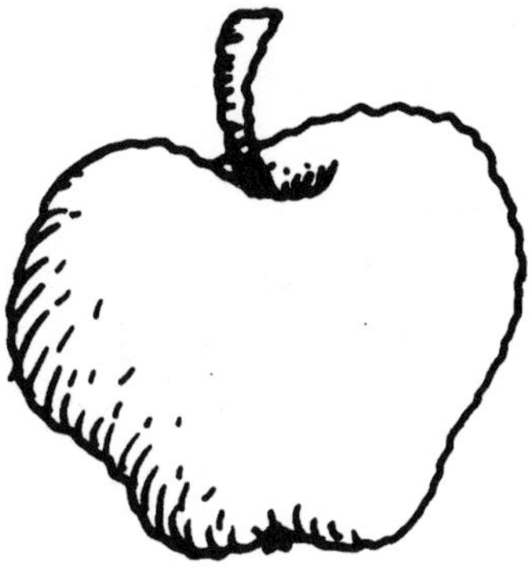
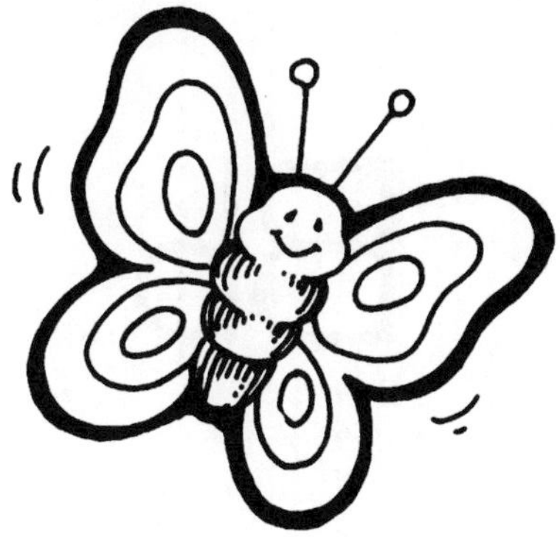
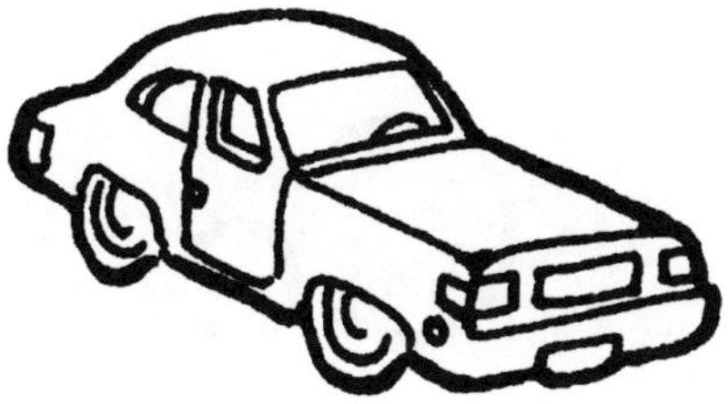
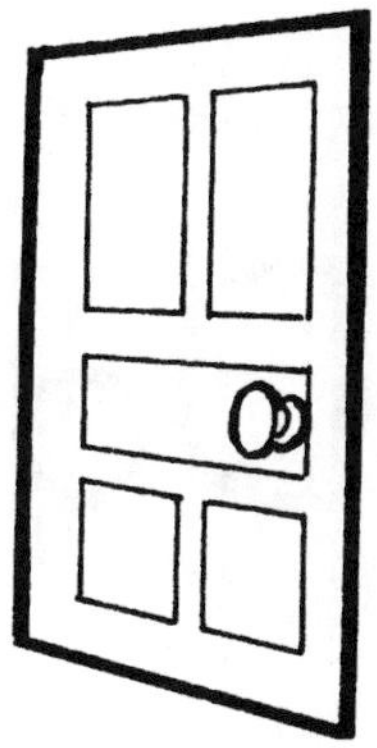
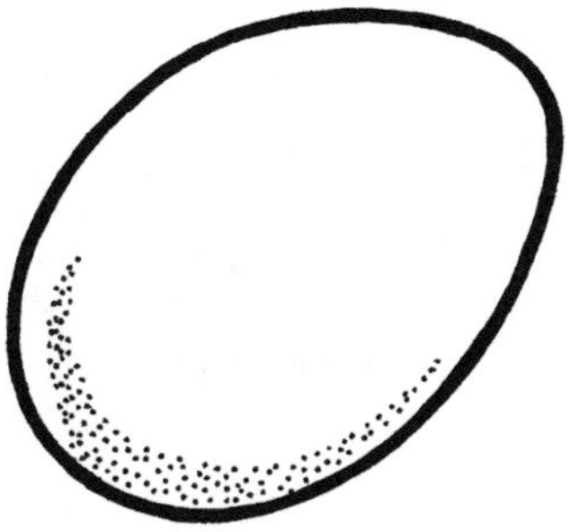
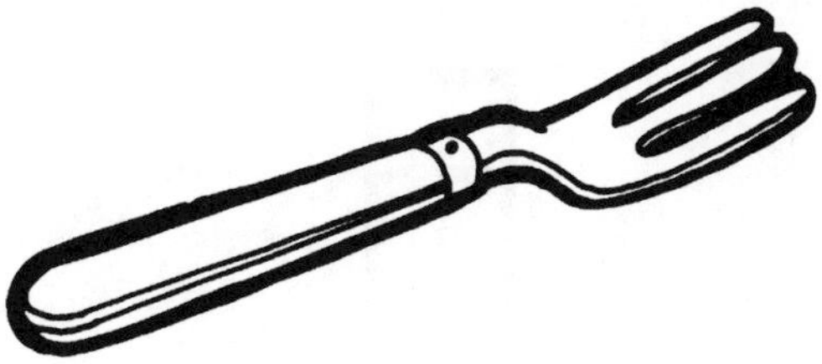
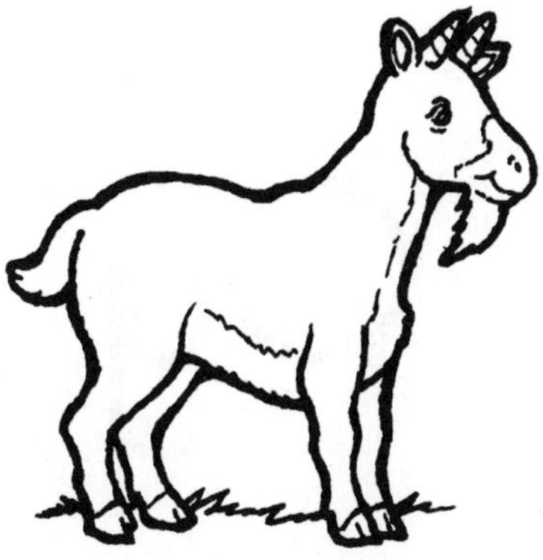
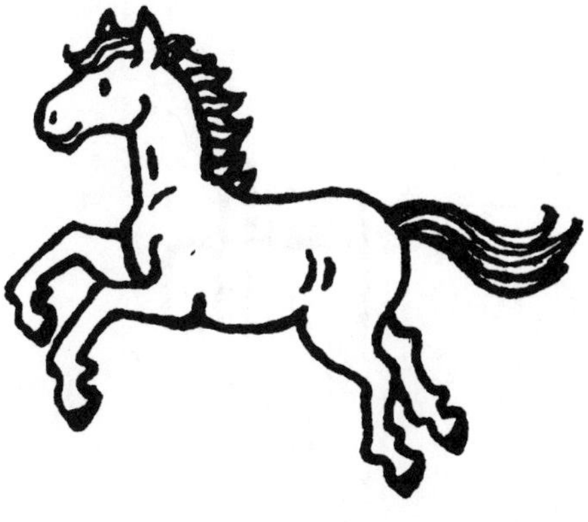

Bb	Aa
Dd	Cc
Ff	Ee
Hh	Gg

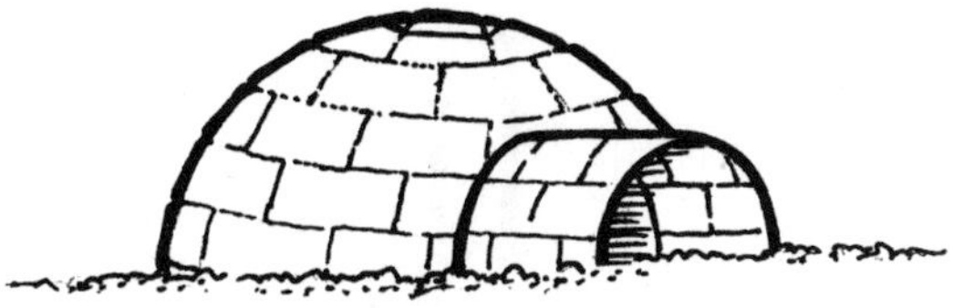

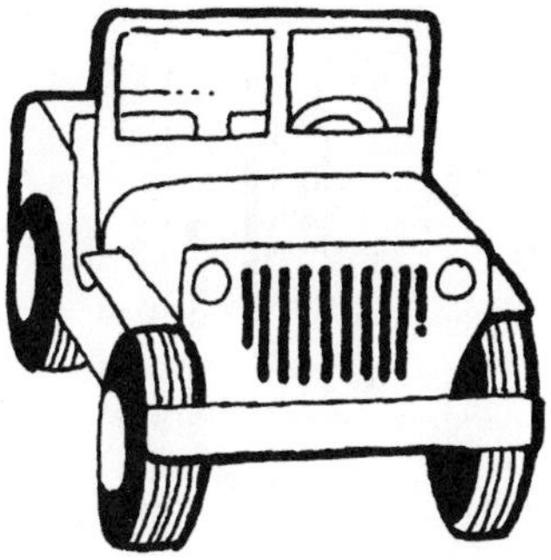

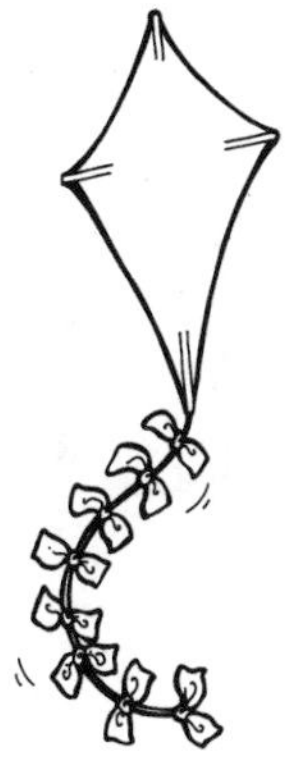

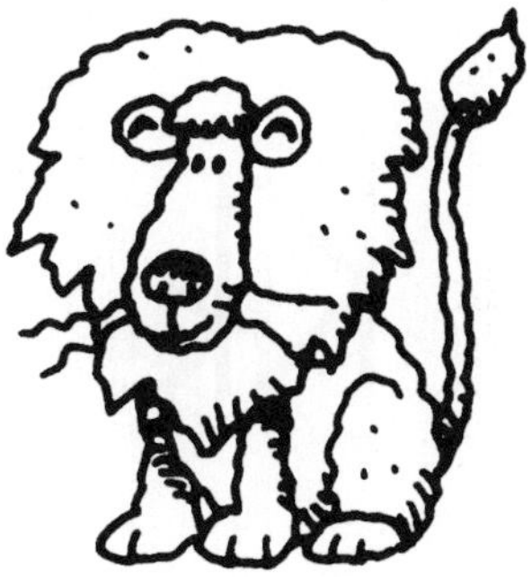

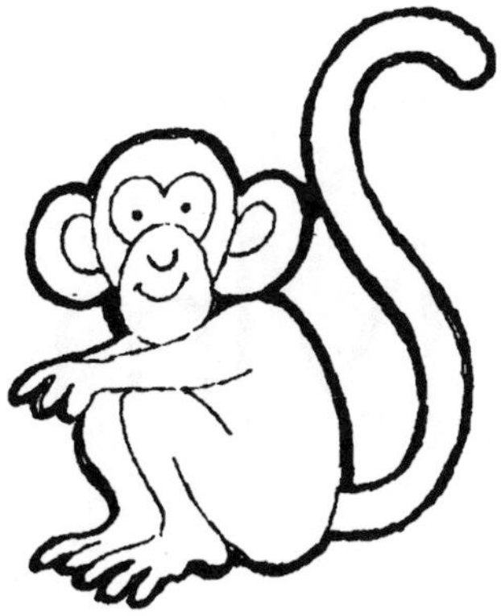

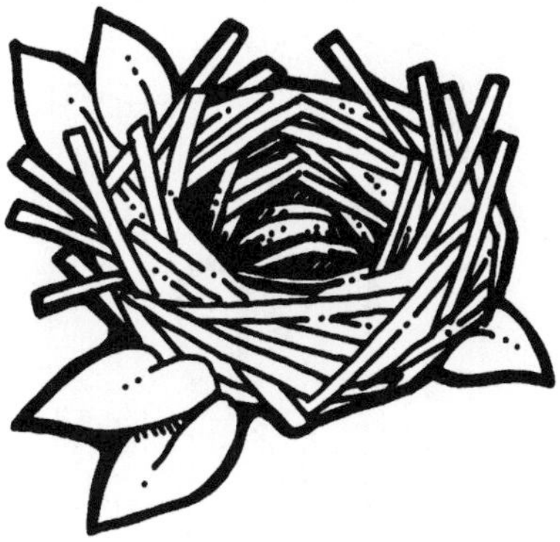

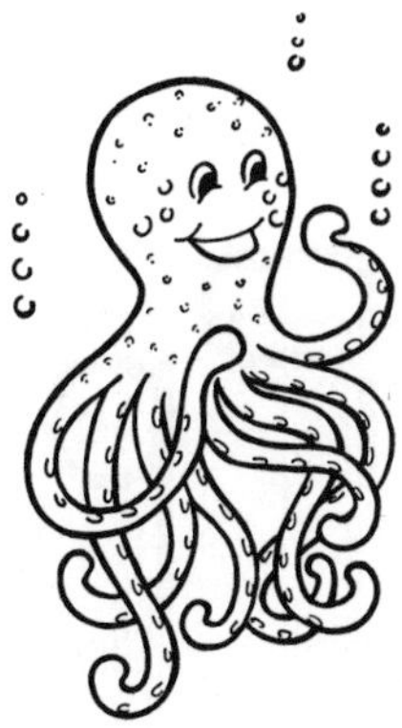

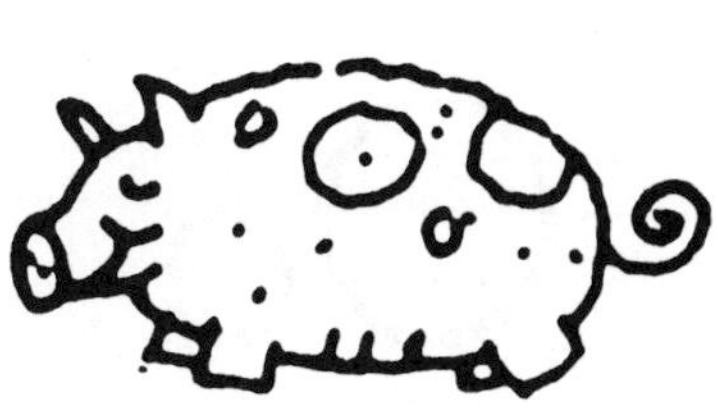

Jj

Ii

Kk

Ll

Nn

Mm

Oo

Pp

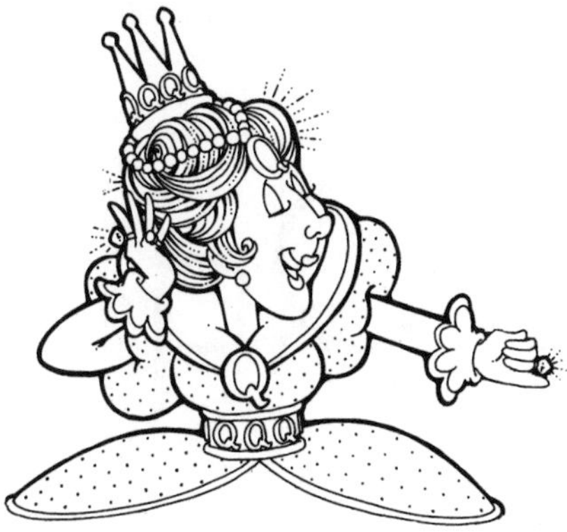

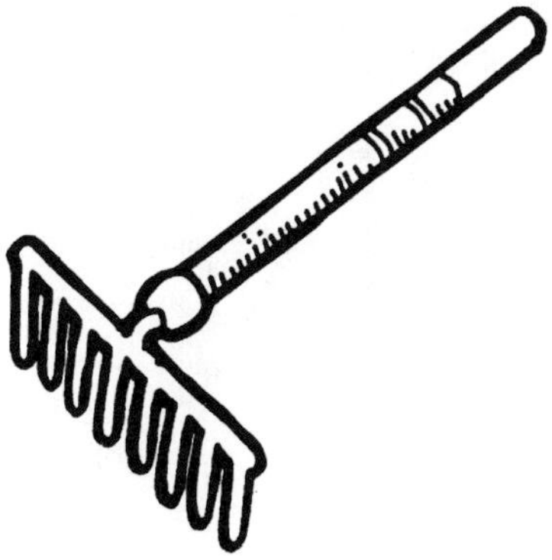

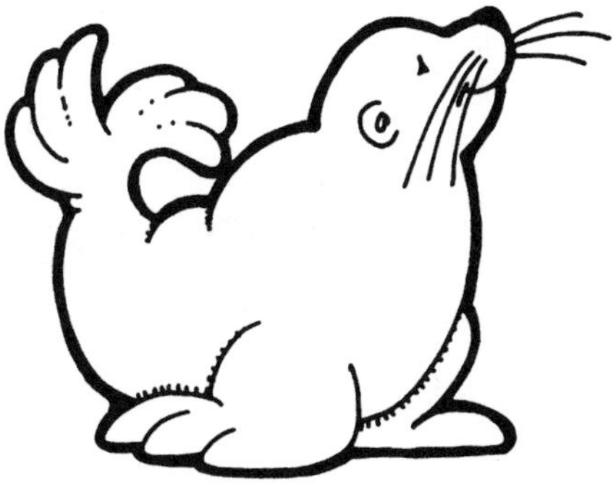

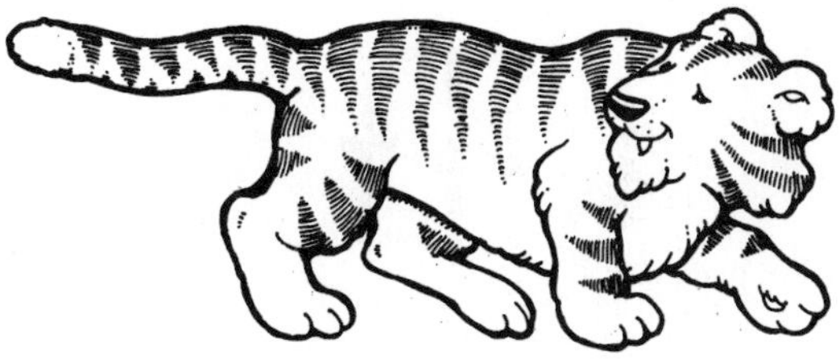

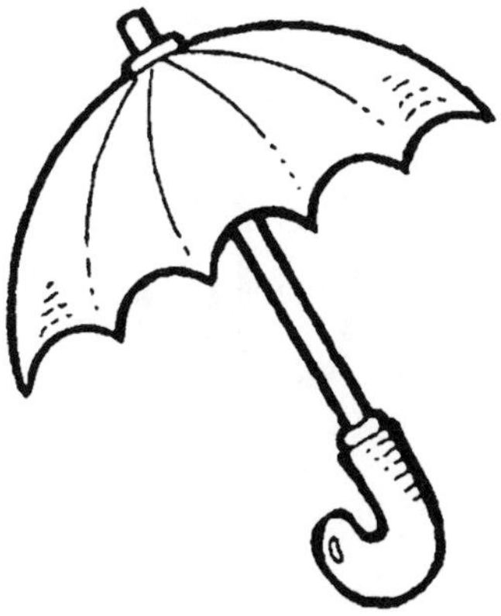

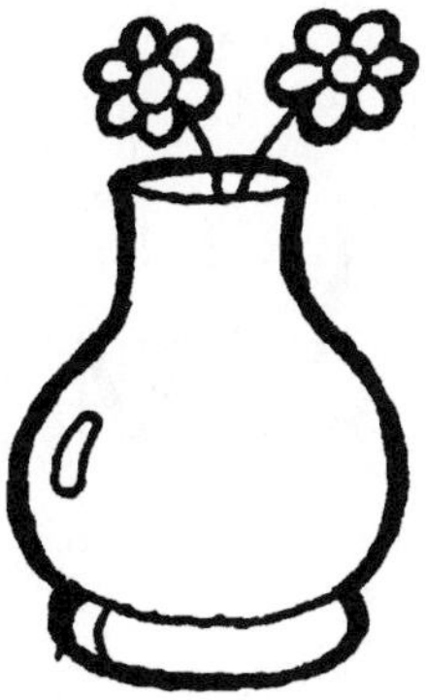

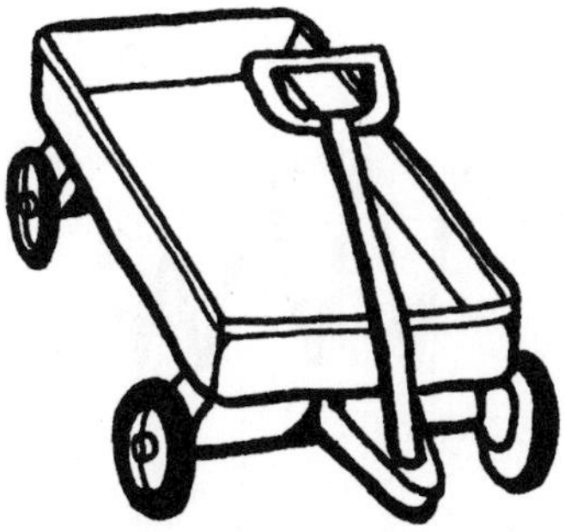

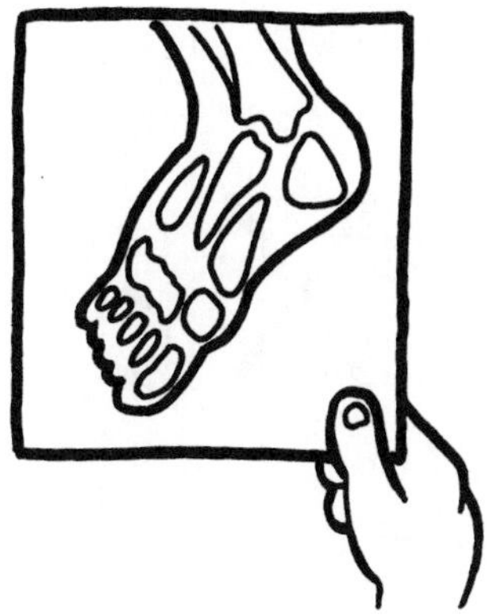

Rr

Qq

Tt

Ss

Vv

Uu

Xx

Ww

a	b	c	d
e	f	g	h
i	j	k	l

Zz

Yy

D C B A

H G F E

L K J I

m	n	o	p
q	r	s	t
u	v	w	x
y	z		

P	O	N	M
T	S	R	Q
X	W	V	U
		Z	Y